D0604474

3080

For Jake and Ben – J.Z.

First edition for the United States, Canada, and the Philippines published in 2004
by Barron's Educational Series, Inc.

Text copyright © Jonny Zucker 2004
Illustrations copyright © Jan Barger 2004

First published in Great Britain in 2004 by
Frances Lincoln Children's Books, 4 Torriano Mews,
Torriano Avenue, London NW5 2RZ
www.franceslincoln.com

All rights reserved.
No part of this book may be reproduced in any form, by photostat,
microfilm, xerography, or any other means, or incorporated into any
information retrieval system, electronic or mechanical, without
the written permission of the copyright owner.

All inquiries should be addressed to:
Barron's Educational Series, Inc.
250 Wireless Boulevard
Hauppauge, New York 11788
http://www.barronseduc.com

Library of Congress Catalog Card No.: 2004104971
International Standard Book No.: 0-7641-2670-9

Printed in Singapore
9 8 7 6 5 4 3 2 1

The Publishers would like to thank Prodeepta Das
for checking the text and illustrations.

Zucker, Jonny.
Lighting a lamp : a
Diwali story /
2004.
33305209225782
cu   01/05/06

FESTIVAL TIME!

Lighting a Lamp

A Diwali Story

Jonny Zucker

Illustrated by Jan Barger

BARRON'S

It's Diwali—the start of the Hindu New Year.
We hear the story about Prince Rama
fighting the demon Ravana to
rescue his wife, Sita.

We put special rangoli patterns
on our doorstep, so that
the goddess Lakshmi will bring us
good luck in the year ahead.

I make delicious sweets
in the kitchen, to enjoy the sweetness
of the Diwali celebration.

We go to the temple to offer prayers and sweets to Rama and Sita.

I exchange gifts and sweets
with all of my friends and cousins.
We look forward to good things
in our New Year.

We light small lamps called diyas,
just as people did to welcome home
Rama, Sita, and Lakshman.

At night there is a brilliant
fireworks display to celebrate
Diwali—our festival of lights.

What is Diwali about?

Diwali, the festival of lights, is one of the most important festivals for Hindus everywhere. It marks the beginning of the new year and symbolizes a renewal of life.

In north India, Diwali celebrates Rama's homecoming, as told in the *Ramayana,* an Indian epic poem. Rama had been banished by his father in order to honor an oath to Rama's stepmother, who wanted her own son to be king. Rama's wife, Sita, and his brother, Lakshman, followed him into the forest, but Sita was abducted by the demon king, Ravana. After fourteen years, Rama returned with his wife and brother to a hero's welcome and took his rightful place as the king. He is believed by Hindus to be an incarnation of God.

In south India, Diwali honors Lakshmi, the goddess of wealth. It celebrates the liberation by Krishna and his wife of thousands of women who had been held by a demon named Narakasura. The festival is celebrated for three to five days, with each day honoring a mythological hero.

Today, Diwali is an occasion for enjoyment. Houses are decorated with **rangoli** patterns (made from colorful rice flour) including motifs of Lakshmi's feet and lotus flowers. People wear new clothes and give sweets to each other. In the south, mothers or grandmothers give everyone in the family a hot oil bath, which is followed by a large, festive breakfast. Firecrackers are lit before sunrise while people pray in the temples. In every home, palace, and place of business, windows, doors, courtyards, and porches are lit up with twinkling little earthen lamps called **diyas**. Today, strings of electric lights are used as well. Noisy fireworks fill the night sky.